Laugh Out Loud

Silly Jokes
for
Kids

ISBN 978-1-64124-317-9

To learn more about the other great books from Fox Chapel Publishing, or to find a retailer near you, call toll-free
800-457-9112 or visit us at *www.FoxChapelPublishing.com*.

We are always looking for talented authors. To submit an idea, please send a brief inquiry to acquisitions@foxchapelpublishing.com.

Fox Chapel Publishing makes every effort to use environmentally friendly paper for printing.

Printed in China
First printing

Laugh Out Loud
Silly Jokes for Kids

Happy Fox BOOKS

Vicki Whiting

Illustrated by
Jeff Schinkel

"We do not take humor seriously enough."

— **KONRAD LORENZ**

What's so funny?

If there's one thing everyone needs, it's a good laugh. And this book can help you make people do just that.

It's filled with jokes that will make you **groan**. And **giggle**. And **guffaw**. And maybe some that cause you to make that weird **SNORK!** sound when you laugh really, really hard!

This book contains jokes about **tigers**, **whales**, **angry citrus**, **ghosts**, **dentists**, **puppets**, **bikes**, **mice**, **worms**, **wizards**, and even **sports-loving potatoes**.

Historians aren't sure who told the world's first joke, or even what that joke may have been about, but there's a good chance it involved a chicken and a road. However, that's **hen**nyone's guess.

See what we did there? We just gave you one extra joke, no extra charge! Sure, it was a groaner. But don't worry! There are plenty of snorks ahead!

What kind of boat takes you to the dentist's office?

The tooth ferry.

Where should you take a seasick boat?

To the nearest doc.

Which vegetables do Navy cooks never use?

Leeks.

How did the marooned sailor wash his clothes?

With tide.

Who was
in the
teacher's
class at
sea?

Buoys and gulls.

How do you
buy a hat
for an
upside-down
boat?

You have to know
its capsize.

What
happened to
the skeleton
that crashed
a rowboat?

It suffered a broken skull.

What happened when a crowd arrived at the boat shop paddle sale?

It was quite an oar deal.

7

What do ghosts put on their mashed potatoes?

What do ghosts put on their bagels?

What kind of pants do ghosts wear?

Grave-y.

Scream cheese.

Boo jeans.

How do you start a letter to a ghost?

"Tomb it may concern."

When do ghosts like to drink a cup of coffee?

What kind of trees do ghosts like best?

When do ghosts go to school?

Early in the moaning.

(Ceme-trees.)

Mondays through Frightdays.

Why don't ghosts like rainy weather?

It dampens their spirits.

What's the difference between lions and tigers?

What's orange with black stripes and goes in circles?

Why is it so tough to be a tiger in the military?

Tigers are missing the mane part.

A tiger on a merry-go-round.

You have to earn your stripes.

If a two-legged animal is a biped, and a four-legged animal is a quadruped, then what is a tiger?

Stri-ped.

10

Why do tigers always eat raw meat?

Why did the kitten try to act like a tiger?

What animal can enter a tiger's den and exit unharmed?

They don't know how to cook.

She was a copycat.

The tiger.

Why are tigers better at hiding than leopards?

Because tigers are never spotted.

What do you get by mixing a pig with a Christmas tree?

A porky pine.

Which holiday do romantic pigs celebrate?

Valenswines Day.

How do pigs send secret messages to one another?

They use invisible oink.

Which hog is the most famous artist?

Pigcasso.

Where do pigs park their cars?

Why did the piglets fall asleep in class?

How did the flying pig miss the airport runway?

In the porking lot.

Their teacher was a real boar.

He came up snort.

How can you get a ticket in a pig pen?

VIOLATION

For running a stop sign.

How do librarians keep warm in winter?

With book jackets.

Why did the baseball player take a bat to the library?

His teacher told him to hit the books.

Who always gets chased in every book?

One page comes after another.

What did the librarian tell the student who checked out a huge stack of books?

"Don't overdue it!"

Why are book writers always cold?

Where do librarians sleep at night?

Why shouldn't you write books on peanut butter?

Because of all the drafts.

Between the covers.

Writing on paper works much better.

What should you do if a shark bites your library book?

AND THE
SEA
HEMINGWAY

Take the words right out of its mouth.

Where can you find cowboy lemons?

Why did the lemon need to keep buying new tires?

What's darker than a lemon?

In the wild, wild zest.

It kept peeling out.

A lem-off.

Why do lemons and limes always get into big arguments?

They are bitter enemies.

Match each riddle with its punch line.

When is it really bad luck to see a black cat?

When you're a mouse.

Why didn't the mouse sign her letter?

She wanted to be anony-mouse.

What's gray, has big ears, and a trunk?

A mouse on vacation.

How do you get a mouse to smile for a photo?

Say "cheese!"

What rodent stole everyone's desserts on the cruise ship?

It was a pie-rat.

How did the mouse feel after taking a bath?

Squeeky clean.

Why do mice prefer to eat shredded cheese?

They think it's really grate.

What kind of automobile insurance do mice have?

Coverage for road dents.

What was wrong with the snowman's computer?

Its screen froze.

What happened when two web pages met?

It was love at first site.

What did the landscaper do when the WiFi routers didn't work?

Mowed 'em.

Why couldn't the computer take off its hat?

Because CAPS LOCK was on!

Why did the chicken cross the internet?

To get to the other site.

Why did the computer go to the eye doctor?

To improve its web sight.

What happened to the computer that fell off the desk?

It broke into PCs.

How did a bird get into the computer?

Someone left a window open.

Why is it no fun playing hide-and-seek with mountains?

They peak.

Why was the camping competition so stressful?

It was in-tents!

How do fleas go for long walks?

They itch-hike.

Can you start a campfire with two identical sticks?

Yes. They're a match!

Where do geologists like to relax?

In rocking chairs.

Why did the bicycle not want to go for a hike in the woods?

It was two-tired.

Why did the rock cry when it heard romantic music?

It was sedimental.

What did the pine tree say to the mountain that kept getting taller and taller?

"Take it easy! Don't you Everest?"

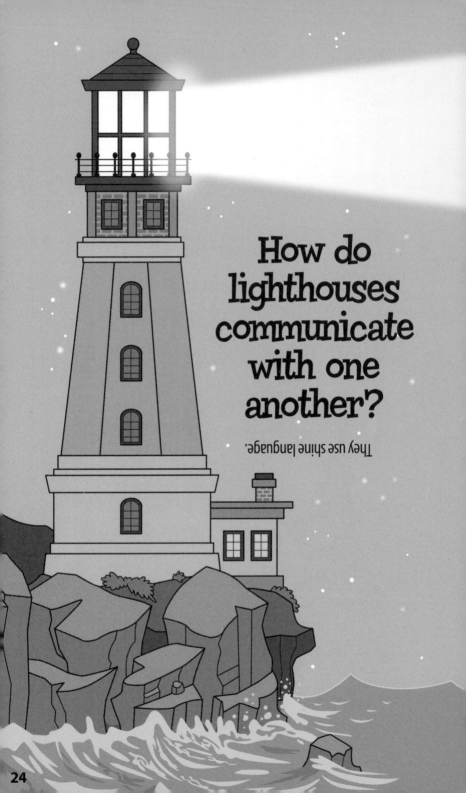

How do lighthouses communicate with one another?

They use shine language.

What instrument do lighthouse keepers play?

Fog horns.

What did the lighthouse keeper make for breakfast?

Beacon and eggs.

What's the difference between a lighthouse keeper and a jeweler?

One watches seas.
The other sees watches.

Why did the actor perform while standing on dictionary?

It was a play on words.

How can you tell when a theater balcony is sad?

When it's in tiers.

Why did the covered wagon start teaching acting?

To be a stage coach.

Why did the actress like to exit through a trapdoor?

It was just a stage she was going through.

What do you get if you mix a sweet potato with a jazz musician?

A yam session!

What do you get by crossing a chicken with a cement mixer?

A brick layer.

Why did the heavy metal band hire the chicken?

The chicken already had drumsticks.

Whose classical music do chickens like best?

Bach! Bach!

What do you get from a chicken with the hiccups?

Scrambled eggs!

Why won't chickens walk under ladders?

When is it the hardest time to find chickens?

Which big city has the largest chicken population?

They think it's bad duck.

On Frydays.

Chick-ago.

Why did the duck cross the road?

To give the chicken directions.

Has anyone ever captured Bigfoot or Sasquatch?

Not Yeti.

Where do unicorn lawyers work?

Unicourt.

Which kind of math do mermaids like best?

Algae-bra.

What do you get by crossing a Yeti and a playground?

A swing and a myth.

How do you make a werewolf giggle?

Why does everyone laugh at giant octopuses'?

What's the best way to meet a sea monster?

Give it a funny bone.

Because they're always Kraken jokes.

Drop it a line!

What's the best way to talk to a giant?

Use a lot of big words.

31

How do you catch an elephant?	Who answers the door at a peanut mansion?	What do peanuts wear on their feet?
Hide in the bushes and make a sound like a peanut.	The peanut butter.	Ca-shoes.

Where does a peanut butter and jelly sandwich leave messages?

On sticky notes.

What did the peanut pirate bury in the sand?

Why is it so easy to share peanut butter?

Which flowers do peanuts like best?

A treasure chestnut.

It spreads all over town.

Buttercups.

What kind of peanuts can travel through space?

Astro-nuts.

What happened to the flight school student who flew into a rainbow during her final test?

She passed with flying colors!

How did the archery team travel to their tournaments?	What kind of chocolate can you buy at the airport?	Why did the pilot get in trouble at flight school?
By arrow-plane.	Plane chocolate.	Bad altitude.

What do you call a plane designed with no wings?

An error-plane.

Why can't Peter Pan work for an airline?

Because he'll never, never land.

What do you get when Dracula is your pilot?

A plane in the neck!

Who invented the world's first paper airplane?

The Write Brothers.

Why do plants avoid math?

They end up with square roots!

How do scientists divide the oceans?

With a sea-saw.

Where do bad rainbows end up?

In prism.

Which dogs do scientists like best?

Laboratory Retrievers.

What music do astronomy teachers like?

Nep-tunes.

Why do DNA scientists look forward to Fridays?

They get to wear their genes to work!

Why should you never pay for dead batteries?

Why are chemistry tests so easy to pass?

Where do magical scientists work?

They're free of charge.

They always have solutions.

In labracadabratories!

Why can't atoms be trusted?

Because they make up everything!

Why couldn't the sponge stop reading the book?

It was so absorbing!

Why did the sponge take so much time reading the newspaper?

To make the moist of it.

What's so great about front doors made of sponge?

You just can't knock them.

What did the homesick sponge say to the Atlantic Ocean?

"Could you be more Pacific?"

How did the sponge and the oyster settle their disagreement?

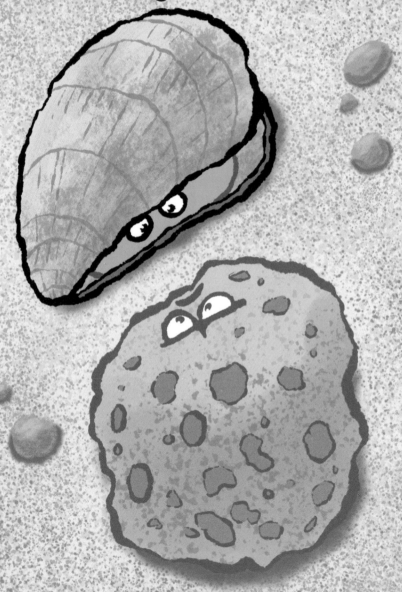

In small clams court.

How do you make a whale float?

Root beer, a scoop of ice cream, and a whale.

How did the whale become rich and famous?

She started a podcast.

What's the best way to help a whale off the beach?

Use a whale-barrow.

Why did the whale have such a messy desk?

She was dis-orca-nized.

Which whales can fly an airplane?

How do whales turn over their pancakes?

What's a whale's favorite lunch?

Pilot whales.

They use their flippers.

A krilled cheese sandwich.

Why did the whale call the police?

She thought she saw something fishy.

What's the best material to use to build a shade structure?

Sun blocks.

What happens to bananas that get a sunburn?

They peel.

What do you call a sunburned librarian?

Well red.

What did the sun say to the blue moon?

"Lighten up!"

42

What does the sun use to serve cold lemonade?

What kind of flowers grow on the sun?

How is the sun like a comic book hero?

Sun glasses.

Ultra violets.

It's a Super Star!

What could happen to Earth if the sun burned out?

Anything's popside.

Why did the dentist take x-rays after meals?

What happens when a dentist takes a vacation?

Where do dentists go on vacation?

To make tooth pics.

They have another dentist fill in.

Flouride-a.

Which dinosaurs have the healthiest teeth?

Floss-iraptors.

What does the Dentist of the Year receive?

A little plaque.

Does everyone smile after a visit to the dentist?

Smileage may vary.

What do orchestra leaders use after every meal?

A tuba toothpaste.

Why did the donuts go to the dentist?

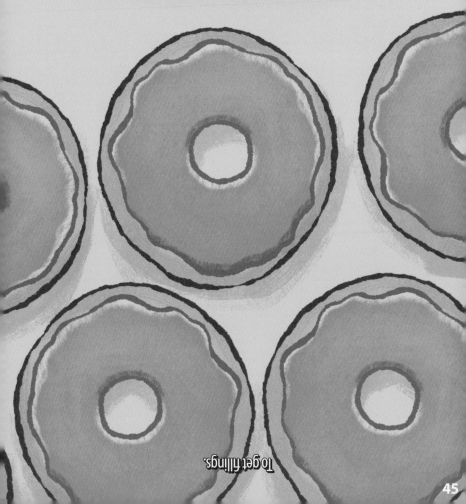

To get fillings.

What do you call a fly without wings?

A walk.

What do you get by crossing a spider with a hamburger?

Patty long legs.

What do you get when you cross an ant with a paper towel?

Absorb-ant.

What does a caterpillar do on New Year's day?

Turns over a new leaf.

What did the flea do when it fell off the dog?

What do insects study in night school?

What kind of bug is Santa Claus most likely to encounter?

What makes lightning bugs glow?

They eat light meals.

What did the quarterback say at the airline ticket counter?

"Put me in coach."

Which team has the coolest helmets?

The one with the most fans.

Why didn't the dog want to play football?

It was a Boxer.

What happened to the football that rolled into the fancy restaurant?

Boogie

It got kicked out.

Which insects are not very good at football?

Fumble bees.

Which football team does Dracula root for?

The Mummy Dolphins.

Why did the football coach shake the gumball machine?

To get a quarter back.

Where did the ghost take the football?

Over the ghoul post.

Who steals soap and shampoo?

What kind of birthday parties do scrub brushes like?

What did the soap give the shampoo when they got married?

Dirty crooks.

Soap-prize parties!

A bathtub ring.

Where do sheep take baths?

In the baaa-aaa-aaa-throom.

Why are rubber duckies in trouble so often?

They're always getting themselves into hot water.

What's the best way to keep mummies clean?

Use bubble wrap.

Why can bathtubs make you feel tired?

Because they're in the restroom.

What happened when the pitcher threw a bar of soap instead of a baseball?

It turned into a bubble play.

Why should you never wear a cardboard belt?

It's a waist of paper!

Why is a camouflage jacket a really smart investment?

It matches everything.

What does every house wear?

A-dress.

What does a cactus wear to the office?

A cac-tie.

How did the underwear begin its speech?

"Let me be brief..."

Why did no one laugh at the clothing designer's jokes?

She needed new material.

Why did the man return his new shoes to the store?

One of the shoes wasn't right.

Why did the house painter have to go out of business?

He kept telling his customers, "It's on the house."

Why did Pinocchio clean the house?

What is the favorite vegetable of marionettes'?

How did the puppeteer meet the king?

What's the best way to make a shadow puppet?

By a show of hands.

54

How do puppets buy cars?

With no strings attached.

Why did the puppeteer hire an assistant?

She needed a helping hand.

What did the angry ventriloquist say to the puppet?

"Speak for yourself!"

Why did the sock puppet quit the theater to go back to its old job?

Because there's no business like shoe business.

Why did the crayon get kicked out of the theme park?

It wouldn't stay in the lines.

Is repairing rollercoasters a good career?

It has its ups and downs.

Did you hear about the guy who rode a carousel for one full year?

He set a whirled record.

What did the carousel horse say on her first day at the theme park?

"I'm new round here."

Which amusement park ride do weasels like best?

The ferret's wheel.

What do you get by leaving potatoes out in the rain?

Spuddles.

How do injured potatoes get to the hospital?

By yam-bulance.

Why do yams wear socks?

To keep their po-ta-toes warm.

What do you call a crowd of potatoes watching a soccer match?

LET'S GO IDAHO! SPUDS #1 TUB

Spec-taters.

What happened to the evil potato that the super hero caught?

Its plans were foiled.

What do you call a yam in a nice hotel?

A suite potato.

Is it fun making mashed potatoes?

Some people find it a-peeling.

Why did the french fries get promoted?

They were overquali-fried.

What does
a worm get
from digging
too many
tunnels?

In-dig-estion.

How do
worms leave
messages
for each
other?

Compost-it notes.

Can you
catch fish
without using
worms?

It's de-bait-able.

What do you get by sending a worm on an around the world cruise?

Global worming.

What do you call a worm without teeth?

A gummy worm.

Why do worms never use alarm clocks?

Because early birds do.

What do you get when you cross a worm, a train, and a big apple?

The New York City subway system.

What did the little worm's mother say when he came home late?

"Where in earth have you been?"

Where can you find leaves shaped like chickens?

On a poul-tree.

When do you know you're out of pancake syrup?

When the maple leaves.

Why did the leaf think he could be elected President?

He had be-leaf in himself.

Which month do trees fear most of all?

Sep-TIMBERRR!

How do trees feel each spring?

Very re-leafed.

What do little bats learn in kindergarten?

The alpha-bat.

Which bats are the most talented?

Acro-bats.

What keeps bats going?

Bat-teries.

How do you decorate a baby vampire's crib?

With a bat mobile.

What do vampire kids do after school?

Just hang out.

Where do vampires serve time for their crimes?

In bat-ting cages.

What is a vampire's favorite sport?

Casket-ball.

How does the vampire carry her books to school?

In her bat-pack.

Do cats
require
a lot of your
money?

No, just a
small purr-cent.

How do
you spell
MOUSETRAP
using only
three letters?

C-A-T.

What
do cats
read first
every
morning?

The mews-paper.

Why can't cats binge
watch TV shows?

They're always on paws.

What is a cat's favorite movie?

The Sound of Mew-sic.

Which flower won the bicycle race?

The one with the most petals.

What do turtles wear when cycling?

A bike shell-met.

What kind of bike will never be haunted by ghosts?

One with no spooks in it.

Why didn't the students finish their drawings of bicycles?

They were two tired.

Why did Kevin ride his bike again and again each day?

He believed in recycling.

What do you need to bike up steep hills?

You should pack a lot of extra gear.

How did the barber win the bicycle race?

Short cut.

What should you do if your dog keeps chasing everyone on a bike?

Take your dog's bike away.

What do you get when you cross a wizard with a blizzard?

A cold spell.

What kind of tests do they give in witching school?

Hex-animations.

Why did the wizard refuse to stop on the freeway?

He won't stop for witch-hikers.

What holds a wizard's book of magic together?

Spell binding.

Why did the witch lose her temper while traveling?

She flew off the handle.

What did the big tube of oil paint say to the little one?

"Don't use that tone with me!"

How
did the artist
paint the row
boat?

Why are
math
teachers
such good
artists?

Would
sea lions
rather swim
or paint?

Stroke by stroke.

A number of reasons.

Art! Art!

How do artists decide who gets to paint first?

They draw straws.

How do you repair broken clouds?

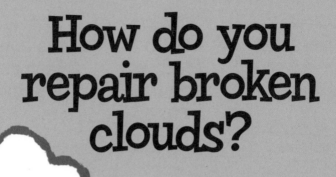

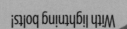
With lightning bolts!

Where did the cloud leave his keys?

He didn't have the foggiest idea.

Where did the rain store its data?

In the cloud.

How come the raindrop couldn't join the storm?

By the time it got there it was already too clouded.

How did the audience react to the cloud's comedy act?

With thunderous applause.

What should you bring to a birthday party in the jungle?

Chimps and dip.

What do monkeys wear when they cook?

Ape-rons.

What are a monkey's favorite flowers?

Chimp-pansies.

What kind of ape can fly?

A hot air baboon.

What
do apes
serve their
guests?

What's the
best month to
find monkeys
in the jungle?

What do you
call an ape
that can't
keep a
secret?

Chimpan-tea.

Ape-ril.

A blab-boon.

What do monkeys learn to write in school?

ABCDE
FGHI
JKLM
NOPQ
RSTU
VWXY
CHIMPANZ

Their ape b c's.

What did the man say when his books fell on his head?

"I blame my-shelf"

What do you get by crossing a library with an airplane?

A fully booked flight.

Why are books afraid of their sequels?

Because sequels are always coming after them!

What's the last part of a book to leave a room?

The end.

Who made this book?

Laugh Out Loud Silly Jokes for Kids was made by the people who bring the weekly *Kid Scoop* page to hundreds of newspapers!

Kid Scoop believes learning is fun! Our educational activity pages teach and entertain. Teachers use the page in schools to promote standards-based learning. Parents use the *Kid Scoop* materials to foster academic success, a joy of learning, and family discussions. Our fun puzzles and activities draw children into the page. This stimulates a child's interest and they then read the text.

When Fox Chapel discovered *Kid Scoop*, they knew that there were lots of kids looking for books just like this one!

Vicki Whiting – Author

Vicki was a third-grade teacher for many years. Now she loves teaching kids through the weekly entertaining and educational *Kid Scoop* page. People often ask where she gets her ideas for each week's page. Vicki says, "I listen to the questions kids ask. We answer those questions with every *Kid Scoop* page!"

Jeff Schinkel – Illustrator

Jeff has loved to draw his whole life! As a kid, sometimes he was drawing when he should have been listening to the teacher in class. He earned a BFA in Illustration at the Academy of Art University in San Francisco, where drawing in class is highly encouraged. Jeff is a member of the National Cartoonists Society.

Eli Smith – Graphic Designer, Webmaster

Eli grew up in Cazadero, California, population 420, near the Russian River. He received a graphics degree from Santa Rosa Junior College and became interested in visual arts through his father, who was a painter. Eli is an accomplished photographer and spends weekends hiking and photographing the hills and beaches of Sonoma County.

Collect them all!

1. Super Silly Jokes for Kids
   978-1-64124-067-3
2. Puzzling Pictures for Eagle-Eyed Kids
   978-1-64124-066-6
3. Super Funny Knock Knock Jokes for Kids
   978-1-64124-142-7
4. Super Fun Road Trip Activities for Kids
   978-1-64124-240-0
5. Mind-Boggling Animal Puzzles for Kids
   978-1-64124-241-7
6. Awesome Funny Fill-Ins for Kids
   978-1-64124-238-7
7. Brain-Bending Animal Puzzles for Kids
   978-1-64124-242-4
8. Super Funny Fill-Ins for Kids
   978-1-64124-239-4
9. Awesome Bird Puzzles for Kids
   978-1-64124-245-5
10. Terrific Travel Fun for Kids
    978-1-64124-243-1
11. Sensational Snow Day Puzzles
    978-1-64124-244-8